BLUE DRAGON

PEACOCK

GREAT WHITE SHARK

SALTWATER CROCODILE

ELEPHANT

DOLPHIN

DECORATOR CRAB

BEARDED VULTURE

ORCHID MANTIS

LEAF-TAILED GECKO

ARCTIC FOX

SEA OTTER

PEACOCK SPIDER

BIRD OF PARADISE

FENNEC FOX

QUOKKA

GALÁPAGOS TORTOISE

SEAHORSE

BIRD OF PARADISE

LION

DRAGONFLY

SKUNK

HOATZIN

PORCUPINE

LIONFISH

SAIGA ANTELOPE

PROBOSCIS MONKEY

DUNG BEETLE

GIRAFFE

AXOLOTL

PANGOLIN

NATIONAL GEOGRAPHIC KiDS

ANIMAL SHOWDOWN

SURPRISING ANIMAL MATCHUPS
WITH SURPRISING RESULTS

★ROUND 2

STEPHANIE WARREN DRIMMER

NATIONAL GEOGRAPHIC
WASHINGTON, D.C.

CONTENTS

BEST DANCER

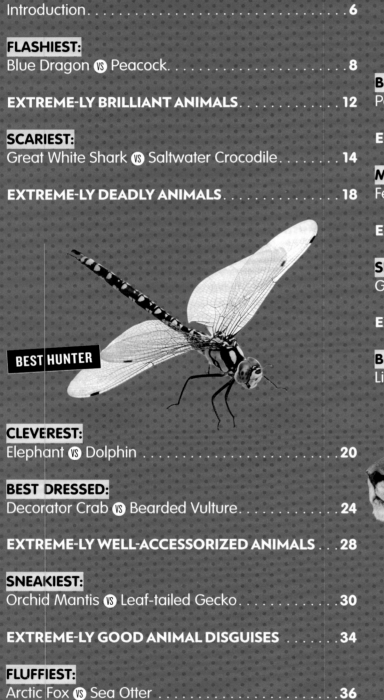

BEST HUNTER

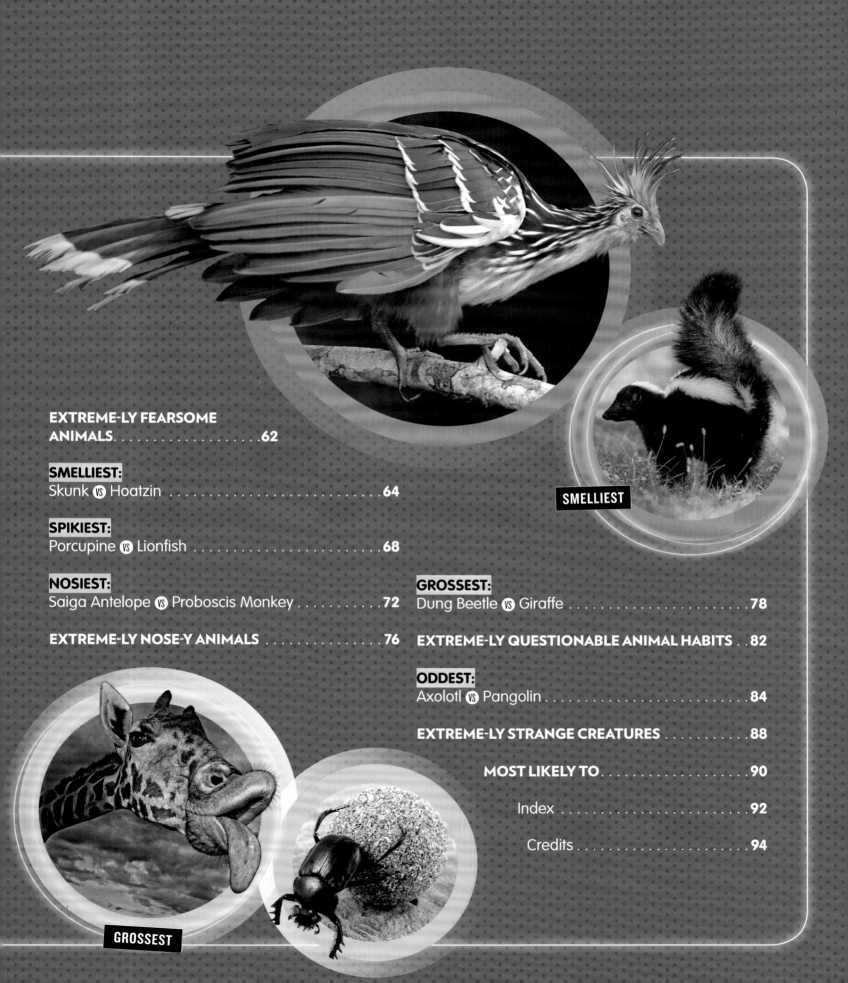

SMELLIEST

GROSSEST

INTRODUCTION

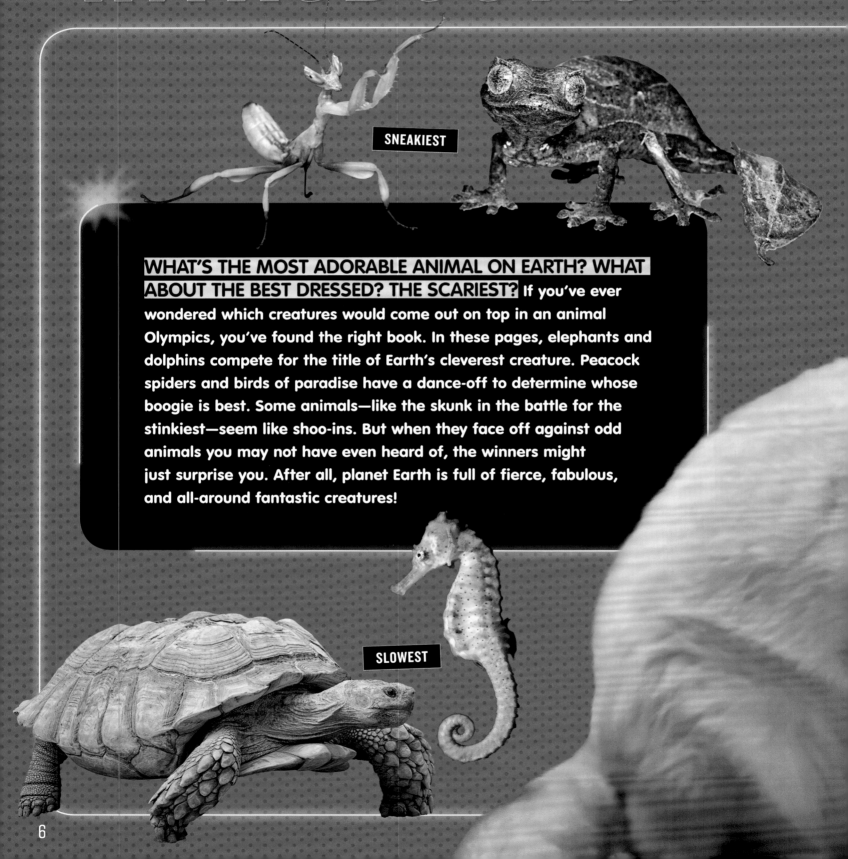

SNEAKIEST

WHAT'S THE MOST ADORABLE ANIMAL ON EARTH? WHAT ABOUT THE BEST DRESSED? THE SCARIEST? If you've ever wondered which creatures would come out on top in an animal Olympics, you've found the right book. In these pages, elephants and dolphins compete for the title of Earth's cleverest creature. Peacock spiders and birds of paradise have a dance-off to determine whose boogie is best. Some animals—like the skunk in the battle for the stinkiest—seem like shoo-ins. But when they face off against odd animals you may not have even heard of, the winners might just surprise you. After all, planet Earth is full of fierce, fabulous, and all-around fantastic creatures!

SLOWEST

FLASHIEST

MOST ADORABLE

SEA STYLE: **BLUE DRAGON**   FANCY FEATHERS: **PEACOCK**

WHO WINS IN THIS SHOWDOWN OF THE SHOWIEST?

One of these creatures is already **FAMOUS** for its **FLASH**, but the **UNKNOWN** up-and-comer could **TAKE THE TITLE!**

BLUE DRAGON

> **THIS CREATURE IS SO STRANGE** it almost doesn't look real. But this is no fairy-tale dragon: The blue dragon is a real-life animal—a type of tiny sea slug that floats through the waters of many of the world's oceans. And its bright blue stripes aren't for looks: They cleverly conceal the animal from surprise attacks.

It's not just the blue dragon's looks that are flashy. This animal has one showy way of defending itself: Its fingerlike appendages are full of venom that can burn any human who dares to touch one. And if you think that's bold, wait until you read how this creature gets its venom!

PEACOCK

> **A PEACOCK'S GLITTERING TRAIN** is one of the most spectacular sights in nature. People have admired peacocks and kept them as pets for thousands of years. Romans decorated their walls with mosaic tile peacocks in the third century. In ancient India, rulers even had their servants fan them with peacock feathers!

It's male peacocks that are known for the fans of blue, gold, and green feathers above their tails. When a male peacock spots a female, called a peahen, he unfurls his train. It forms a semicircle up to seven feet (2 m) across! He vibrates it, making the iridescent feathers flash in the light. It's a dazzling display!

BLUE DRAGON ★ VS ★ PEACOCK

WHICH ANIMAL WILL FLAUNT ITS WAY TO THE WIN?

AN **AIR BUBBLE** IN THE BLUE DRAGON'S STOMACH KEEPS IT **AFLOAT.**

CLEVER CAMO
Blue dragons float around upside-down. Their blue belly faces upward, where it is camouflaged against the blue ocean to predators looking down from above. Their silvery back faces down so animals looking up from below can't see the critter against the bright surface of the water.

BOTH MALE AND FEMALE BLUE DRAGONS CAN PRODUCE EGGS. How cool is that? Spiral in shape, the **EGGS FLOAT THROUGH THE WATER OR LAND ON A NEARBY SURFACE,** where they hatch.

STOLEN STINGERS
The blue dragon loves to eat stinging creatures like the Portuguese man-of-war, a deadly, jellyfish-like ocean drifter. But the blue dragon doesn't just snack on this critter—it also steals its stinging cells, called nematocysts. It collects huge amounts of nematocysts in its skin, making the blue dragon many times deadlier than the man-of-wars it snacks on.

BLUE DRAGON

WINNER

| COMMON NAME: | BLUE DRAGON | SCIENTIFIC NAME: | GLAUCUS ATLANTICUS |

SIZE:

1–1.5 INCHES (3–4 CM)

WHERE THEY LIVE:
THE ATLANTIC, PACIFIC, AND INDIAN

OCEANS

When a peacock quivers his train for a potential mate, the feathers make a sound too low for humans to hear. **PEACOCKS CAN CHANGE THE SOUND THEY MAKE BY SHAKING DIFFERENT PARTS OF THEIR FEATHERS** to attract females at different distances. Jazzy trick!

CRYSTAL POWER

The peacock's feathers owe their bright colors to tiny, crystal-like structures. They're so minuscule that each one is hundreds of times thinner than a human hair. The way these color crystals are spaced determines what shade of light they produce.

MATING GAME

A peacock's enormous fan has no practical function: It's totally for show! But why would a creature carry around such a bulky body part? The question puzzled scientists until 2002, when one study found that the healthier the bird, the more fabulous his fan. The tails let the females know which male peacock will make the strongest father.

PEACOCK

COMMON NAME: **PEACOCK**	SCIENTIFIC NAME: **AFROPAVO, PAVO**

SIZE:

WHERE THEY LIVE:

UP TO **9.1** FEET (2.8 M)

AFRICA, INDIA,
SRI LANKA, JAVA, AND MYANMAR

A GROUP OF PEACOCKS IS SOMETIMES CALLED A **PARTY.**

Peacocks are famous for their showy feathers. But though they don't have the same fan following, blue dragons, with their brilliant blue hues, are a strong competitor. When it comes to flash factor, they've got the edge on the peacock: Blue dragons not only eat some of the sea's most dangerous animals, they turn their prey's poison into their own defense! **WINNER: BLUE DRAGON.**

EXTREME-LY BRILLIANT

BRILLIANT ANIMALS

TRULY BRILLIANT

The blue dragon and the peacock may boast blazing displays of color. But these animals are SO FLASHY, THEY ACTUALLY GLOW IN THE DARK!

FIREFLY

The animals most famous for their **GLOW**, fireflies produce a **CHEMICAL REACTION** inside their bodies that makes light, a trick called **BIOLUMINESCENCE.**

SCALY DRAGONFISH

This strange fish has a **LONG TENTACLE** dangling from its chin. **THE TIP GLOWS**— probably to attract prey—**LIKE A LIGHT-UP FISHING ROD.**

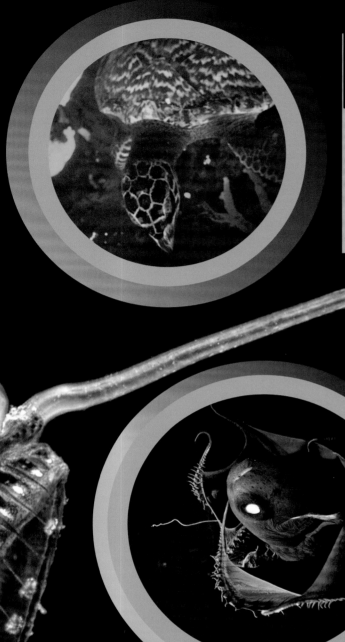

In 2015, scientists caught something new on film: a sea turtle **GLOWING GREEN, RED, AND ORANGE.** Before that, nobody knew sea turtles could do this—and experts aren't yet sure of the reason!

CLUSTERWINK SNAIL

Merely being bioluminescent isn't good enough for this sea snail. These clever crustaceans have **CRYSTALS IN THEIR SHELLS** that act like magnifying glasses, amplifying their glow to make it **LOOK LIKE IT'S COMING FROM A MUCH BIGGER CRITTER.**

VAMPIRE SQUID

Many squids squirt ink when attacked to distract their predators. But that strategy doesn't work too well in the deep, dark sea. The vampire squid **RELEASES A CLOUD OF GLOWING MUCUS** instead.

LANTERNFISH

Out of my way! The lanternfish **LIVES IN THE DEEP SEA, WHERE THERE'S NO SUNLIGHT.** But that's no problem: **IT HAS A HEADLAMP, AN ORGAN ON ITS SNOUT THAT LIGHTS THE WAY.**

SCARIEST

YOU WOULDN'T WANT TO ENCOUNTER EITHER OF THESE TERRIFYING PREDATORS IN THE WILD.

Both have **MIGHTY JAWS** and a mouthful of **SUPERSHARP TEETH**.
But who wins the title of Earth's **SCARIEST** animal?

GREAT WHITE SHARK

❯ **THERE'S NO DOUBT WHO RULES** the open ocean. Great white sharks are the planet's largest predatory fish, some reaching more than 20 feet (6 m) in length—as big as a dump truck!

Great whites are some of the best hunters on the planet, and they use the element of surprise to do it. When it spots its intended prey on the surface of the water, a great white will swim underneath. Then, using its massive tail like a propeller, it lunges upward with such speed and power that it bursts out of the water, snagging the animal in its jaws. That seal never stood a chance!

SALTWATER CROCODILE

> **CROCODILES SEEM SCARY,** but the truth is, most species would rather flee from people than attack. There's one supersize exception: the saltwater crocodile. These highly aggressive predators can reach jaw-dropping proportions—some are more than 23 feet (7 m) long!

And these crocs mean business. When hunting prey, they lie submerged under the water's surface. They can hold their breath for more than an hour, making for one scary sneak attack. When an unsuspecting animal gets close, the croc uses its powerful hind legs and tail to lunge. Then—SNAP!

GREAT WHITE SHARK
★ VS ★
SALTWATER CROCODILE

We wouldn't want to be caught in the water near either of these **BLOODCURDLING BEHEMOTHS!**

GREAT WHITES DON'T CHEW THEIR FOOD. INSTEAD, THEY **RIP** THEIR PREY TO PIECES AND SWALLOW THOSE WHOLE.

GREAT WHITE SHARK

COMMON NAME: **GREAT WHITE SHARK** SCIENTIFIC NAME: **CARCHARODON CARCHARIAS**

SIZE:

2.5 TONS (2.3 T) OR MORE

WHERE THEY LIVE:

COOL, **COASTAL WATERS** AROUND THE WORLD

TERRIFYING TEETH
Great whites have 300 sharp, serrated teeth in their mighty jaws. And if they lose one, no big deal: If one tooth falls out, another moves forward from their rows of backup teeth. A great white can go through some 20,000 teeth in a lifetime!

As if this predator wasn't scary enough already, great whites **HAVE A SIXTH SENSE CALLED ELECTRORECEPTION, WHICH HELPS THEM HUNT DOWN THEIR PREY.** Special sensors in the skin on their snouts can **DETECT THE ELEC-TRICAL CURRENTS GIVEN OFF BY ALL LIVING CREATURES.** This allows them to even hunt down animals that are hiding under the sand on the seafloor.

SNIFFING OUT PREY
Great whites use their exceptional sense of smell to track down prey. Their noses are so sensitive that they can sniff out one drop of blood in 25 gallons (95 L) of water.

SALTWATER CROCODILE

| COMMON NAME: | SALTWATER CROCODILE | SCIENTIFIC NAME: | CROCODYLUS POROSUS |

SIZE:

MALES CAN BE AS BIG AS
2,200 POUNDS (1,000 KG)

WHERE THEY LIVE:

INDIA, SOUTHEAST ASIA, AND NORTHERN
AUSTRALIA

BIG BITE

When a saltwater croc opens its mouth, it's a frightening sight. Their jaws are filled with more than 60 teeth up to five inches (13 cm) long. And those teeth snap together with a force of 3,700 pounds per square inch (260 kg/sq cm)—the strongest bite of any animal ever recorded.

LAND AND SEA

Saltwater crocs might be at home in the water, but you can't escape them by staying on dry land: While they normally stay along coastal regions, they've been spotted swimming some 30 miles (48 km) offshore in the open ocean—and they also come on shore to bask in the sun and lay their eggs.

Saltwater crocs will EAT JUST ABOUT ANYTHING. They regularly snack on TURTLES, SNAKES, AND BIRDS. And larger males aren't afraid to go after huge animals like WATER BUFFALO—OR HUMANS. Saltwater crocs are so aggressive that they'll even EAT ANOTHER CROC if it gets too close.

SCIENTISTS THINK SALTWATER CROCODILES BITE WITH ABOUT THE **SAME FORCE** AS THE MIGHTY TYRANNOSAURUS REX ONCE DID.

WINNER

Though many people think of great white sharks as man-eaters, the odds of dying by shark attack are extremely low: just one in 3.7 million. You're more likely to be killed by an asteroid! But saltwater crocs are different. Though it's still rare, they attack humans about 25 times each year—and an estimated 40 percent of those attacks are fatal. Some say saltwater crocs are the animal most likely to kill a human. We say that makes them the scariest animal on the planet. **WINNER: SALTWATER CROCODILE.**

EXTREME-LY DEADLY ANIMALS

PLANET EARTH IS BRIMMING WITH SWEET, CUDDLY CREATURES. THESE ... AREN'T THEM.

Meet six more biting, stinging, charging, and **JUST PLAIN TERRIFYING** animals.

AFRICAN BUFFALO
⌄They're **NICKNAMED THE BLACK DEATH** for a reason. When threatened, African buffalo will charge at up to 35 miles an hour (56 km/h), and are known to continue the attack even when injured.

BOX JELLYFISH
⌃It's the **MOST VENOMOUS MARINE ANIMAL IN THE WORLD.** Box jellyfish can have tentacles up to 10 feet (3 m) long, covered with thousands of stingers. The venom is so toxic that many people die before they can swim back to shore for help.

MOSQUITO
The world's **MOST DEADLY ANIMAL** is also one of the **SMALLEST.** Just about 0.1 inch (2.5 mm) long, they carry diseases to nearly every corner of the planet, slaying an astounding 725,000 people each year.

CONE SNAIL
This tropical snail is prized for its beautiful, brown-and-white shell. But don't get too close: It has a sharp, **VENOMOUS STINGER EQUIPPED WITH POWERFUL PARALYZING POISON.**

BLACK MAMBA
IT'S SPEED THAT MAKES THE BLACK MAMBA SO FRIGHTENING. These snakes can slither at speeds of up to 12.5 miles an hour (20 km/h), nearly as fast as the fastest human sprinters. And if a bitten person doesn't receive the right medicine within 20 minutes, the mamba's bite is fatal.

GOLDEN POISON DART FROG
These colorful frogs have **POISON IN THEIR SKIN SO POTENT THAT ONE FROG HAS ENOUGH TO KILL 10 ADULT MEN.** Indigenous people of South America have been using it on the tips of their blow darts for centuries.

CLEVEREST

THINK *HUMANS* ARE THE *SMARTEST* ANIMALS ON *EARTH?*

Read on and you might be **SURPRISED** at just how **CLEVER** these two creatures can be!

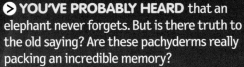

ELEPHANT

▶ **YOU'VE PROBABLY HEARD** that an elephant never forgets. But is there truth to the old saying? Are these pachyderms really packing an incredible memory?

Research says the rumors are true. Some elephants live in the desert where water is scarce. The females that lead the herds show an amazing ability to keep track of all the watering holes in their territory and take the shortest route between them—even when they are located hundreds of miles apart! Older elephants can even remember tough conditions from the past—like drought—and use those memories to help the herd survive—like leading them to remote watering holes. But elephants don't just have stellar memories: They exhibit many other signs of deep intelligence, too.

DOLPHIN

❯ SPOTTING SMARTS CAN BE TRICKY when the creature in question is totally different from us. Dolphins communicate with clicks. They use echolocation to "see" underwater. They sleep by resting one half of their brains at a time. But though they're nothing like humans, a host of research shows that dolphins are among Earth's most intelligent animals. They have big brains relative to their body size—nearly as big as humans'. Like humans, they live in tight-knit social groups. They whistle, click, and chirp to each other constantly beneath the waves. Many scientists believe they're using these vocalizations to communicate—but what they're saying is a mystery.

ELEPHANT VS DOLPHIN ★ ★

THESE SURE ARE SOME SMART ANIMALS. Wouldn't it be nice if they could do your math homework?

ELEPHANTS CAN **USE TOOLS—** THEY'VE BEEN OBSERVED STACKING BLOCKS INTO A MAKESHIFT STEP STOOL TO REACH A TREAT HUNG UP HIGH.

THEY FEEL COMPASSION

Elephants comfort each other when distressed, stroking an anxious companion with their trunks. They will help babies climb out of holes. And they will assist injured companions—even pulling out tranquilizer darts!

When they come across the REMAINS OF A DEAD COMPANION, elephants exhibit behaviors not seen in any other animal. They STROKE the bones gently with their trunks and sometimes STAND with the body for days. They've even been seen COVERING dead comrades WITH SOIL OR LEAVES.

THEY FORM CLOSE BONDS

In 1999, an elephant named Jenny reacted with extreme excitement when a new elephant named Shirley arrived at her refuge in Tennessee, U.S.A. Workers investigated and found out that the two had performed at the same circus for a few months—22 years earlier! The reunited pair became best buds.

ELEPHANT

COMMON NAME:	ELEPHANT	SCIENTIFIC NAME:	ELEPHANTIDAE FAMILY

SIZE:
5,000 TO
14,000 POUNDS
(2,268–6,350 KG)

WHERE THEY LIVE:
AFRICA AND **ASIA**

THEY HAVE NAMES

Dolphins use special sounds called signature whistles like humans use names—to call to and identify each other. It's thought that dolphins invent these whistles for themselves when they're young. Dolphins can recall a companion's signature whistle after being separated for decades.

THEY PLAY

Many experts think playing is a strong sign of intelligence. Dolphins have been spotted riding boat wakes like surfers, playing catch by throwing a fish or turtle back and forth, and even competing in high-speed games of tag.

To keep her tank **CLEAN,** trainers rewarded a captive dolphin named Kelly with a **FISH** whenever she brought them a **PIECE OF TRASH** that had fallen in. So Kelly started hiding pieces of **PAPER UNDER A ROCK** in the water. When the trainer came along, Kelly would **TEAR OFF PIECES** and bring them to the surface one by one—turning one treat into many!

DOLPHIN

| COMMON NAME: | DOLPHIN | SCIENTIFIC NAME: | DELPHINIDAE FAMILY |

SIZE:

WEIGHING ABOUT
500 POUNDS
(227 KG)

WHERE THEY LIVE:

IN OCEANS
AND SOME RIVERS AROUND THE WORLD

DOLPHINS CAN USE TOOLS. SOME PLACE SEA SPONGES ON THEIR SNOUTS, PROTECTING THEM FROM JABS FROM STONEFISH AND STINGRAYS AS THEY LOOK FOR FOOD ON THE SEAFLOOR.

It's hard to peer inside an animal's mind and figure out just how smart it is. But it's certain that both elephants and dolphins are highly intelligent. Just like humans, both creatures live in complex social groups, which means using their smarts to get along with others. But some scientists think that dolphins are the second-smartest animals on the planet, after us. **THAT MAKES DOLPHINS SQUEAK THEIR WAY TO THE WIN!**

BEST DRESSED

STYLISH SHELL: **DECORATOR CRAB** FASHIONABLE FEATHERS: **BEARDED VULTURE**

YOU MIGHT THINK HUMANS HAVE A MONOPOLY ON THE *FASHION DEPARTMENT.*

After all, we're the only species that **ADORNS OURSELVES WITH ACCESSORIES ... right?** Wrong. Meet planet Earth's **TWO BEST-DRESSED BEASTS.**

DECORATOR CRAB

❯ IF YOU EVER SEE a piece of the seafloor get up and start walking, take a closer look. You might actually have spotted a decorator crab! These chic crustaceans collect items they find, such as seaweed, sponges, and corals, and stick them to their shells. Tiny hooked hairs act like Velcro, holding everything in place.

You might accessorize to stand out, but decorator crabs do it for the opposite reason: to blend in. The crabs' decorated shells perfectly mimic the ocean floor, making it tough for predators like fish and octopuses to spot them. No dying for fashion here!

DECORATOR CRAB VS BEARDED VULTURE

BEARDED VULTURE

> **BEARDED VULTURES** live a mostly solitary life high in the mountaintops. Since each guards a territory 77 to 154 square miles (200–400 sq km), they're rarely spotted. But even though they don't have much of an audience, they put a lot of thought into their outfits. Adult bearded vultures naturally have snow-white feathers … which the birds dye blood-red!

The creepy color might seem fitting when you consider their lifestyle: A bearded vulture's diet is 70 to 90 percent bone—the only animal known to live this way. After other scavengers have made a kill, the vulture swoops in to snag a bone. It carries its meal high into the air, then lets loose, aiming for a rock below. The bone hits the rock and shatters, revealing the juicy marrow within. With a diet like that, it's a little surprising these birds bother to dress up for dinner!

WHICH ANIMAL WINS THIS FACE-OFF of the most fashionable?

SCIENTISTS PUT POM-POMS INTO TANKS WITH DECORATOR CRABS—AND THE CRABS STUCK THE COLORFUL CRAFT SUPPLIES ALL OVER THEMSELVES!

DECORATOR CRAB

COMMON NAME:	DECORATOR CRAB	SCIENTIFIC NAME:	MAJOIDEA FAMILY

SIZE:

UP TO **5** INCHES
(12.7 CM)

WHERE THEY LIVE:

SHALLOW WATERS
WORLDWIDE

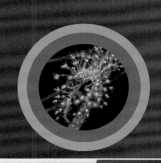

TOXIC THREADS

Some decorator crabs are picky about their outfits: They select specific shell accessories that will ward off predators, like stinging anemones and poisonous seaweed. Even if predators spot the crabs, they'll think twice about attacking.

When decorator crabs **SCUTTLE INTO A NEW TERRITORY,** they sometimes **FIND THAT, suddenly, THEIR SPONGES AND ANEMONES LOOK OUT OF PLACE IN THEIR NEW HOME.** That's no problem: The crabs simply **PULL OFF THEIR OLD DECORATIONS** and **STICK ON SOME NEW ONES THAT BLEND IN BETTER.**

THIS OLD THING?

Like all crustaceans, decorator crabs have to shed their shells when they grow too big for them. But they don't want to waste their old outfits. So the crabs carefully pick off their corals and sponges and place them on the new shell. Thrifty!

For a long time, scientists **DIDN'T KNOW HOW BEARDED VULTURES GOT THEIR BOLD RED HUE. They finally got** answers in 1995, when wild vultures were spotted **ROLLING AROUND IN MOUNTAIN POOLS LACED WITH REDDISH, RUSTY IRON DEPOSITS.**

STATUS SYMBOL

Bearded vultures have no predators, so their cosmetics can't be for camouflage. Instead, some scientists think they're a message to other vultures. Bigger, older birds tend to have deeper hues from lots of color applications. Those could signal that they're so skilled at finding food, they have free time to work on their appearance.

PROTECTIVE PAINT

When you spend your life rooting around in carcasses, bacteria can be a big problem. Some scientists think bearded vultures' decoration has a function: Bathing in iron oxides may kill disease-causing microbes. The red pigment might be the vulture equivalent of hand sanitizer!

BEARDED VULTURE

COMMON NAME: **BEARDED VULTURE** SCIENTIFIC NAME: **GYPAETUS BARBATUS**

SIZE:

WINGSPAN OF
8.9 FEET (2.7 M)
HEIGHT OF 3.8 FEET (1.16 M)

WHERE THEY LIVE:

MOUNTAINOUS AREAS FROM
EUROPE TO CHINA
TO AFRICA

THE BEARDED VULTURE IS THE ONLY BIRD IN THE WORLD KNOWN TO **DECORATE** ITSELF.

Decorator crabs sport fashion that isn't just for looks—it helps keep them from becoming a stylish sea snack. Bearded vultures' fashion is functional, too: Their red feathers may help them communicate with other birds or protect them from nasty microbes. But while the birds only accessorize with red pigments, the crabs get creative. They use anything they can get their claws on, including other sea creatures! That makes their outfits just a little more impressive.

WINNER: DECORATOR CRAB.

EXTREME-LY

WELL-ACCESSORIZED ANIMALS

SOME ANIMALS HAVE A SERIOUS SENSE OF FASHION.

You might think they're WEIRD—but nature thinks they're FABULOUS.

MAGNIFICENT FRIGATEBIRD

When it comes time to **ATTRACT A MATE**, the male magnificent frigate-bird **KNOWS HOW TO PUT ON A SHOW.** He inflates his bright red throat sac, clatters his bill, and shakes his head back and forth. **ATTRACTIVE!**

BLANKET OCTOPUS

Unlike most of their kind, blanket octopuses **DON'T LIVE ON THE SEAFLOOR,** where there are lots of crevices for squeezing into. So they have to **CARRY AROUND THEIR OWN PROTECTION:** webs between their long arms that they fan out to scare predators.

ATLANTIC SAND FIDDLER

These crabs look like they'd be right at home in a sports stadium, waving their one giant claw for their favorite team. **BUT THEY ACTUALLY USE THEIR OVERSIZE APPENDAGE**—usually four times bigger than the other—**TO DEFEND THEIR BURROWS.**

STALK-EYED FLY

After the male stalk-eyed fly emerges from its pupa, it gulps in air, then pumps it into the stalks on its head, **BLOWING THEM UP LIKE BALLOONS.** Why the extraordinary eyes? Scientists aren't sure!

GUM LEAF SKELETONIZER CATERPILLAR

When most caterpillars get too big for their hard outer **EXOSKELETONS,** they simply shed them and move on. Not this creepy caterpillar. Instead of discarding its outgrown skulls, **IT STACKS THEM ON TOP OF ITS HEAD,** and wears them around like a hat.

MARKHOR

This goat relative has perhaps the most **SPECTACULAR HEADGEAR** on the planet. Its **SPIRAL HORNS** can grow to more than five feet (1.5 m) in males. When fighting over females, markhors lock their horns together and twist.

SNEAKIEST

THESE ANIMALS ARE MASTERS OF DISGUISE!

No, you're not looking at a **BEAUTIFUL FLOWER** or a **DEAD LEAF**. These animals have perfected the **ART OF CAMOUFLAGE**.

ORCHID MANTIS

❯ **IT'S PERHAPS THE MOST STUNNING** insect on Earth. With its pink and white colors and its delicate, petal-like limbs, the orchid mantis uses its entire body to mimic a flower—the first creature known to do so. It may be beautiful—but it's also a vicious hunter. Mantises can strike in just .031 second— nearly three times faster than a human's punch!

Many living things copy their surroundings to hide in plain sight. At first, that's what scientists thought the orchid mantis was doing—waiting among the flowers until an unsuspecting bug came along. But it turns out that this insect's hunting strategy is even sneakier than that ...

LEAF-TAILED GECKO

> **THIS CRITTER MIGHT LOOK CREEPY.** And if cornered, this lizard will open its mouth to show the bright red inside, call loudly, flap its tail, and stare down its foe with its menacing glare.

But even though they can put on a show, these creatures prefer to avoid confrontation by not being seen in the first place. This is where their incredible disguise comes in. Leaf-tailed geckos manage to look just like another dead leaf in their tropical forest homes. Just like leaves, their bodies are mottled brown in color, have curved bodies that mimic the shape of a leaf—and even have skin marked with lines that look like leaf veins. That's quite the camouflage!

FORGET A WIG AND A FAKE MUSTACHE. These two animals are the real experts at concealing their identity.

SOME MANTISES **CATCH** AND **EAT** HUMMINGBIRDS.

ORCHID MANTIS

WINNER

COMMON NAME:	ORCHID MANTIS	SCIENTIFIC NAME:	HYMENOPUS CORONATUS

SIZE:

FEMALES
2.4 INCHES
(6 CM)

MALES
1.2 INCHES
(3 CM)

WHERE THEY LIVE:

SOUTHEAST
ASIA

FLOWER POWER
Orchid mantises don't wait for prey to stumble into their grasp. Instead, insects actually fly right to the mantis. Why? Experts realized that mantises don't camouflage themselves among flowers. Instead, their whole body mimics a flower. Hungry insects come flying in for a flower snack. Then, gulp!

ORCHID MANTISES ARE BORN WHITE. But they can detect the conditions around them— like **HUMIDITY AND LIGHT LEVELS—AND CHANGE THEIR COLORS TO PINK AND PURPLE** to mimic the flowers that grow in their area. Nifty trick!

NINJA MOVES
When its victim comes close, it's game over. Mantises have lightning-fast arms that they can use to snag their prey in just about 60 milliseconds—that's about four times faster than the time it takes you to blink your eye!

The most incredible part of the gecko's **DISGUISE IS ITS TAIL**. It's not only shaped and colored like a leaf, but it also has **IMPERFECTIONS AND MISSING CHUNKS** that make it look exactly like it has begun to **ROT AWAY OR HAS BEEN NIBBLED ON BY INSECTS**.

EXTREME NAPPING

These geckos like to spend the day snoozing. Some curl up among the leaves on the forest floor, twisting their bodies and wrapping their tails around themselves to look more leaf-like. Others like to hang off of tree branches from their grippy hind feet.

NIGHT STALKER

These reptiles rest during the day. But when the sun sets, it's time to hunt. Their huge eyes help them spot prey in the darkness. Scientists aren't sure what these geckos prowl for, but they think the lizards probably eat anything they can swallow, from spiders to crickets.

LEAF-TAILED GECKO

| COMMON NAME: | LEAF-TAILED GECKO | SCIENTIFIC NAME: | UROPLATUS PHANTASTICUS |

SIZE:

UP TO
6 INCHES
(15.2 CM) LONG

WHERE THEY LIVE:

MADAGASCAR,
AFRICA

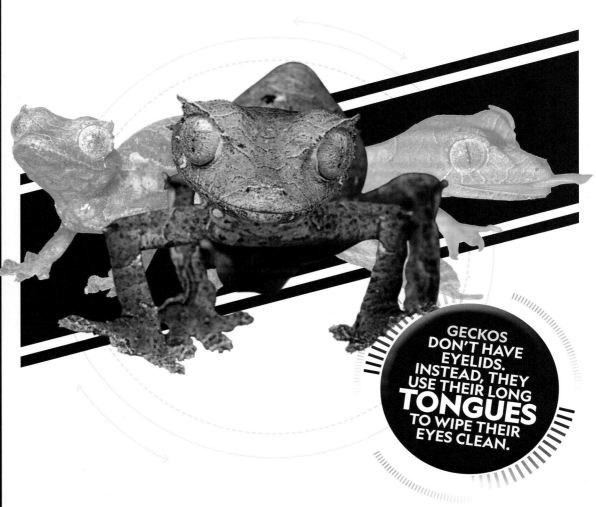

GECKOS DON'T HAVE EYELIDS. INSTEAD, THEY USE THEIR LONG **TONGUES** TO WIPE THEIR EYES CLEAN.

Both sneaky creatures are marvelous mimics. Millions of years of evolution have shaped the mantis's legs into delicate flower petals and the gecko's tail into a perfectly decaying leaf. So which one has the edge? **WE HAVE TO GIVE THE WIN TO THE ORCHID MANTIS.** Its disguise is so convincing, the mantis's meal comes right to it. That's what you call dinner delivery!

EXTREME-LY GOOD ANIMAL DISGUISES

THESE MASTERS OF CAMOUFLAGE MAKE BLENDING IN AN ART FORM.

Can you **SPOT** these animals **HIDING** in **PLAIN SIGHT?**

SAND VIPER

This scary snake wiggles its body to **BURY** itself in the sand of its African desert home. With just its eyes peeking out, it's **NEARLY IMPOSSIBLE** to see!

EASTERN SCREECH OWL

During the day, this owl finds a hole in a tree and positions itself inside. Like a **MAGIC TRICK**, its feathers seem to fill the hole, **BLENDING** the owl right into the bark around it.

BARON CATERPILLAR

⌄ Good luck spotting this butterfly larva clinging to a leaf in western Malaysia. It's got a good reason to hide: If it can avoid being eaten, it will **TRANSFORM** into a baron butterfly.

CUTTLEFISH

⌃ This sea creature sports what is perhaps the **MOST ELABORATE DISGUISE** in the animal kingdom. Every square millimeter of its skin has up to **200 COLOR-CHANGING CELLS.** Below those are muscles that can morph its skin to mimic the texture of nearby rocks or reefs.

STICK INSECT

⌄ Most animals need to hold still in front of a particular backdrop for their camouflage to hide them. But the **STICK INSECT,** which **LOOKS LIKE PART OF THE TREE** it climbs on, is concealed wherever it goes.

LICHEN SPIDER

⌃ Looking just like the lichen-covered trees it likes to rest on, this spider stays **FROZEN** in place, waiting to **AMBUSH** unwitting insects.

FLUFFIEST

FUZZY ON LAND: **ARCTIC FOX**   FURRY BY SEA: **SEA OTTER**

IT'S A MATCHUP OF THE **SOFT** AND **FUZZY!**

Both these animals are known for their **CUDDLY COATS**—
but which truly deserves the title of **FLUFFIEST**?

ARCTIC FOX

> WHEN WINTER ARRIVES IN THE ARCTIC, things get cold—really cold. Blowing snow and blinding winds are everyday conditions. But unlike humans, animals can't stay inside and order a pizza when the weather turns nasty. The arctic fox hunts through the frigid season. Luckily, it has an excellent winter coat!

In the winter, the arctic fox grows thick, warm fur to protect it from the cold air. The fur is longer on the fox's chest and belly to help protect the animal from the chill when the critter lies down on the snow. With this incredible coat, the arctic fox can survive through truly glacial temperatures of minus 94°F (-70°C).

SEA OTTER

> **MOST OCEAN ANIMALS KEEP WARM** with a layer of blubber underneath their skin. But watch a walrus rolling around on the beach and you'll see that all that blubber isn't the most graceful way to keep out the cold. The sea otter does things differently: It uses a specially-designed fur coat to keep warm beneath the waves.

Sea otters have incredibly luxurious fur: They can have nearly one million hairs per square inch (150,000 hairs/sq cm). In comparison, the average human has about 100,000 hairs on their entire head! That dense coat keeps sea otters comfortable in the frigid waters along the North Pacific coasts where they live.

How best to choose a winner? **TOO BAD WE CAN'T JUST HUG THESE CONTESTANTS IN THIS CONTEST FOR THE FLUFFIEST!**

TO HUNT, ARCTIC FOXES **LISTEN** FOR ANIMALS **SCURRYING** UNDER THE SNOW.

ARCTIC FOX

COMMON NAME:	ARCTIC FOX	SCIENTIFIC NAME:	VULPES LAGOPUS

SIZE:

UP TO

27 INCHES
(69 CM) LONG, WITH A 14-INCH (36-CM) TAIL

WHERE THEY LIVE:

THE ARCTIC

SEASON SHIFT
Unlike your winter coat, an arctic fox's can change with the weather: In summer, their fur is brown or gray to match the rocky ground. In winter, it turns pure white to blend in with the snow.

SNUGGLE UP
Like a cat's, the arctic fox's tail helps it keep its balance as it runs and leaps across the tundra. But the fox's tail—also called a brush—has a more adorable function, too: When the fox gets chilly, it wraps its tail around its face like a scarf. *Aww!*

THE ARCTIC FOX'S COAT HAS TWO LAYERS: Beneath the long outside hairs, there is **ANOTHER LAYER OF SOFT HAIRS** tightly packed together. This system **TRAPS A LAYER OF WARM AIR NEXT TO THE SKIN** to keep the fox warm in the Arctic winters.

A SEA OTTER'S COAT IS ALSO MADE UP OF TWO LAYERS: The inner layer TRAPS AIR TO KEEP IT WARM and is protected by a layer of long guard hairs. The outer layer is so thick it KEEPS THE WATER FROM TOUCHING THE OTTER'S SKIN.

HIGH MAINTENANCE

To keep their coats waterproof, otters spend many hours a day grooming themselves. When they're not primping, they're mostly eating. Otters like to float on their backs, using their chests like a table to crack open clams and mussels.

LITTLE OTTERS

At birth, otter pups' fur makes them so buoyant they can't dive underwater! Pups bob on the surface while the mother otter hunts for food. Sometimes, she wraps the end of a strand of kelp around her baby to make sure it doesn't float away while she's gone. How sweet!

SEA OTTER

WINNER

| COMMON NAME: | SEA OTTER | SCIENTIFIC NAME: | ENHYDRA LUTRIS |

SIZE:

4 FEET LONG (1.2 M)

WHERE THEY LIVE:

NORTH PACIFIC OCEAN

SEA OTTERS WERE ONCE NEARLY HUNTED TO **EXTINCTION** FOR THEIR COATS, BUT NOW THEY'RE **PROTECTED!**

It's a close call in this cuddly critter competition. But when it comes to choosing the fluffiest, it's all about the fur facts: While an arctic fox has an impressively dense coat with about 130,000 hairs per square inch (20,000/sq cm), **A SEA OTTER HAS NEARLY ONE MILLION HAIRS PER SQUARE INCH (150,000/SQ CM). THAT GIVES IT THE THICKEST COAT IN THE ANIMAL KINGDOM—AND EARNS IT THE WIN!**

BEST DANCER

GET READY TO BOOGIE.

The **PEACOCK SPIDER** and the **BIRD OF PARADISE** both sport flashy costumes and strut their stuff in some of nature's most incredible displays. It's a **DANCE-OFF** of the animal kingdom!

PEACOCK SPIDER

> **THESE SPIDERS,** found in parts of Australia, are truly itty-bitty: Most species are around an eighth of an inch (3 mm) long. But these tiny dancers have big moves. They perform a dance perhaps more intricate and flashy than any other on Earth.

When a male peacock spider spots a female, he raises his third pair of legs high in the air and waves them rhythmically, like a disco dancer. He hops from side to side, shaking his body back and forth. And he always performs for an audience: A female spider closely watches each spin and sway. He's counting on his skills on the dance floor to impress her.

PEACOCK SPIDER VS BIRD OF PARADISE

BIRD OF PARADISE

❯ **THEY WAVE PLUMES** that resemble rust-colored dusters. They wiggle what look like feathered antenna and raise what appear to be iridescent shoulder pads. They hop, jiggle, and sing. They're the birds of paradise, a group of birds that have some of the most seriously impressive dances on Earth.

Not many people get to see their treetop tangos: These birds live only in the rainforests of New Guinea and on a few remote islands of Australia. But even though their performances are rarely spotted, the beautiful colors and elaborate rituals of their courtship boogie have earned them big reputations.

WHICH CREATURE WILL WALTZ ITS WAY TO A WIN?

SCIENTISTS **NICKNAMED** TWO NEW PEACOCK SPIDER SPECIES DISCOVERED IN 2015 SPARKLEMUFFIN AND SKELETORUS.

FAN FAVORITE
Peacock spiders get their name from the brilliantly colored fan attached to their abdomens. When they start their dance, they unfurl the fan and wave it from side to side, hoping to dazzle their potential mate with its flashy colors and patterns.

GIVE ME A BEAT
The peacock spider doesn't just dance; he makes his own music, too! During his routine, he drums on the ground with his legs. The vibrations travel across the ground and are picked up by sense organs in the female's legs. Hopefully she likes the music!

PEACOCK SPIDER

WINNER

COMMON NAME:	PEACOCK SPIDER	SCIENTIFIC NAME:	MARATUS GENUS

SIZE:

⅛ INCH (3 MM) ON AVERAGE

WHERE THEY LIVE:

AUSTRALIA

For these tiny spiders, **DANCING IS A LIFE-OR-DEATH ACT.** If the male suitor's dips and spins **DON'T IMPRESS HIS POTENTIAL MATE, SHE DOESN'T JUST WALK AWAY—SHE EATS HIM!** Scientists say it's only the **BAD DANCERS THAT BECOME DINNER.** Talk about motivation to perfect your moves!

BIRD OF PARADISE

| COMMON NAME: | BIRD OF PARADISE | SCIENTIFIC NAME: | PARADISAEIDAE FAMILY |

SIZE:

RANGES FROM
5.9 INCHES
(15 CM) TO 43 INCHES (109 CM) FOR
ONE BIRD WITH A VERY LONG TAIL

WHERE THEY LIVE:

THE RAINFORESTS OF
NEW GUINEA
AND A FEW ISLANDS IN AUSTRALIA

IT'S ALL FOR HER

Male birds of paradise want their moves to impress the ladies: Watchful females choose the best dancers to mate with. Over millions of years, that's created birds of paradise with increasingly intricate choreography.

Birds of paradise don't make up their moves on their own. They INHERIT THEIR COURTSHIP DISPLAYS FROM THEIR FATHERS. Years before they get their adult feathers, young males start to practice their skills. They even TEST OUT THEIR CHOREOGRAPHY FOR OTHER MALES. How are my moves, dude?

FLAUNT THOSE FEATHERS

In most parts of the world, donning such flashy finery would be a sure way to get eaten. But these birds live on islands where there aren't many predators. They can show off vibrant feathers and jazzy dances with no risk—so they do.

THE PAROTIA BIRDS OF PARADISE FORM A **TUTU** SHAPE WITH THEIR FEATHERS, LEADING THEIR MOVES TO BE CALLED THE BALLERINA DANCE.

So which critter has the best boogie? There's no doubt that birds of paradise have their prance perfected. From their elaborate feathery costumes to their amazingly complex congas, they seem to have thought of everything when it comes to showing off their best moves. But if the female doesn't like their dance, she just flies away. The stakes are a lot higher for the peacock spiders—they literally dance for their lives! **WINNER: PEACOCK SPIDER.**

EXTREME-LY COOL ANIMAL MOVES

ON THE HUNT FOR SOME NEW DANCE MOVES?

Look no further than the animal kingdom. These creatures can SAMBA, DISCO, and FOX-TROT with the best of them.

CLARK'S GREBE

When two of these birds pair up, they SYNC THEIR DANCE MOVES, too. They move together through a sequence of MIRRORED MOVES, ending with a grand finale called "the rush." Together, they speed across the surface of their pond, MOVING SO FAST THEY ACTUALLY RUN ON WATER!

SEAHORSES

Every morning, male and female seahorses across the oceans come together for a SUNRISE TANGO. They SWIM SIDE BY SIDE, spinning and dipping. Sometimes, they even HOLD TAILS! Now that's true romance.

SPANISH DANCER

It may be a **SEA SLUG,** but this marine animal is no slouch in the dance department. Spanish dancers move by **RIPPLING THE EDGES OF THEIR MANTLE.** In combination with their **DEEP RED COLOR,** this gives them the appearance of a **FLAMENCO DANCER'S SWIRLING SKIRT.**

SHREW

Shrews have big families—up to seven youngsters at a time. When they need to keep everyone together, they do it in style: They **FORM A CONGA LINE,** with each little shrew **BITING THE TAIL OF ITS SIBLING IN FRONT.**

SIFAKA

These **LEMURS** of Madagascar have **SHORT ARMS** and **LONG LEGS**— good for **LEAPING** through treetops, not so good for walking on all fours. Instead, when on the ground, they move by gracefully **PRANCING** on two legs, holding their arms out for **BALANCE LIKE BALLERINAS.**

BLUE-FOOTED BOOBY

Put your blue foot in, put your blue foot out ... during mating rituals, male blue-footed boobies **STRUT** around to **SHOW OFF THEIR FEET** to the females. **THE BLUER HIS FEET, THE MORE LIKELY SHE IS TO FIND HIM ATTRACTIVE!**

MOST ADORABLE

IT'S A CLASH OF THE CUTEST!

A **TEENY-TINY FOX** with great big ears takes on a **FURRY MARSUPIAL** famous for its sweet smile. Which will come out on top?

FENNEC FOX

❯ **IT'S THE SMALLEST** of all the world's foxes, weighing in at a petite 2.2 pounds (1 kg). But the fennec fox has ears so large, at 6 inches (15 cm) long, they look like they belong to a much bigger critter! Pair those outsize ears up with a soft, furry coat and you have one adorable animal.

Sometimes called desert foxes, these dainty desert-dwellers make their home in the hot and sandy zones of North Africa and the surrounding areas. There, fennec foxes forage for anything edible in their dry, hot home: from plants to eggs to rodents. To beat the heat, they spend the day underground, then emerge at dusk to hunt during the cool nights. Cute *and* clever!

FENNEC FOX VS QUOKKA
★ ★

QUOKKA

> **EVERY YEAR,** more than 500,000 tourists flock to one small island, called Rottnest, off the coast of Australia. They're there to see the quokkas, relatives of the kangaroo and about the size of a house cat. About 10,000 of these furry critters—almost all the quokkas in the world—live on the island.

With their fluffy bodies and teddy-bear-shaped ears, quokkas are already cute from a distance. But get close enough, and you'll see the feature that makes people travel far and wide to see them: Quokkas sport a natural grin! The sweet smile has earned quokkas the nickname "world's happiest animal."

BOTH ANIMALS ARE TINY, FURRY, AND DOWNRIGHT ADORABLE—so which cute critter will earn the win?

THE FENNEC FOX'S **FURRY FEET** MAKE GREAT **SHOVELS** FOR DIGGING THEIR UNDERGROUND DENS.

FENNEC FOX

COMMON NAME:	FENNEC FOX	SCIENTIFIC NAME:	VULPES ZERDA

SIZE:

9–16 INCHES (23–41 CM) LONG

WHERE THEY LIVE:

THE SAHARA AND THE DESERTS OF NORTH AFRICA

ENORMOUS EARS
There's no question, the fennec fox's oversize ears are its cutest quality. But they're not just for looks. Fennec foxes use their ears to listen for prey hiding underground. The big ears also act like built-in air conditioners: They radiate body heat to keep the foxes cool in their hot home.

Wearing a **FUR COAT IN THE DESERT** might seem like a bad idea. But the fennec fox's fur **PROTECTS THEM FROM THE SCORCHING SUN** during the day, and also **KEEPS THEM WARM** when desert temperatures drop at night. The fox even has **FURRY FEET**, which act like **SNOWSHOES (OR RATHER, SAND SHOES)** to help the fox walk on the desert sand!

SANDY SNOOZERS
During hot desert days, fennec foxes choose to stay out of the sun—and take a nap instead! They dig dens up to three feet (1 m) deep in sand dunes to make a cozy sleep spot. Though they're considered solitary animals, sometimes two foxes will connect their dens. It's nice to have a nap buddy!

BIG GRIN

People travel from all over the world to visit the quokkas. And the quokkas seem happy to see them, too! Though they're usually nocturnal, many quokkas like to stay awake during the day when tourists are around. The quokkas aren't truly smiling—it's just how their mouths are shaped—but they sure look delighted to have company!

IT'S HOPPENING

Though they might resemble a tiny bear, quokkas are actually cousins of the kangaroo. Like their larger relatives, they carry their babies in pouches on their stomachs. And quokkas hop, too—surely the most *aww*-inspiring way to get around!

Until 2012, most people outside Australia had **NEVER HEARD OF THE QUOKKA.** Then, a visiting tourist **TOOK A SELFIE** with one of the grinning critters, and the snap went viral. Since then, people have flocked to get their own quokka selfies. The attention has helped the quokkas—which are considered **VULNERABLE TO EXTINCTION—** begin to bounce back.

QUOKKA

WINNER

| COMMON NAME: | QUOKKA | SCIENTIFIC NAME: | SETONIX BRACHYURUS |

SIZE:

16–21 INCHES
(41–53 CM) LONG

WHERE THEY LIVE:

SOUTHWESTERN
AUSTRALIA

QUOKKAS LIKE TO **NAP IN THE SHADE** IN GROUPS DURING THE DAY.

This one's tough! Judged on looks alone, no one could choose between fennec foxes and quokkas in a matchup for the world's most adorable animal. So it comes down to personality. And a quokka's charisma is undeniable—just look at those jolly faces! **WINNER: QUOKKA.**

EXTREME-LY *CUTE ANIMALS*

SAY AWWWW!

EARTH IS HOPPING, WADDLING, and WIGGLING
with all kinds of **ADORABLE ANIMALS.**
You may have never heard of some of these
creatures, but one of them just might be
your new favorite animal.

AMAZON RIVER DOLPHIN
◀ They chirp and chortle, they leap out of the water—
AND THEY'RE PINK! These dolphins live in the Amazon
and Orinoco river basins of South America.

DIK-DIK
◀ These African antelopes are truly tiny—some
weigh just seven pounds (3.2 kg)! To communicate,
**THEY WHISTLE THROUGH THEIR NOSES, MAKING
A NOISE THAT SOUNDS LIKE "DIK-DIK."**

MEERKAT

> Meerkats have an adorable habit: **STANDING TALL ON THEIR HIND LEGS TO WATCH OUT FOR PREDATORS, USING THEIR TAILS FOR SUPPORT—** just like a kickstand on a bike.

CHAMELEON

∧ Can a reptile be cute? With their mitten-like hands, curled tails, and rolling eyes, chameleons are undeniably adorable. The smallest chameleons, called *Brookesia micra*, **ARE SO TEENY THEY CAN SIT ON THE HEAD OF A MATCH!**

HARP SEAL

Until they're two weeks old, harp seals have fluffy, bright white coats. **THIS HELPS CAMOUFLAGE THESE ANIMALS AGAINST THE ICE OF THEIR ARCTIC HOME.**

LITTLE PENGUIN

< If you thought penguins couldn't possibly get any cuter, think again! **THE SMALLEST OF ALL PENGUIN SPECIES,** little penguins are just 13 inches (33 cm) tall.

SLOWEST

LUMBERING ON LAND: **GALÁPAGOS TORTOISE**   SLUGGISH AT SEA: **SEAHORSE**

READY, SET, GO... HELLO?

It's a **RACE** for **LAST PLACE** in this showdown of the **SLOWEST** animals on Earth.

GALÁPAGOS TORTOISE

❯ **THESE CREATURES ARE SO SLOW** that they're famous for it! Giant Galápagos tortoises, the biggest of their kind on the planet, can be longer than five feet (1.5 m) and weigh 550 pounds (250 kg)—about as much as a ride-on lawn mower!

They're also some of the slowest animals around, traveling about 130 to 160 feet (40 to 50 m) in an entire day. These huge animals simply aren't in a hurry: Adult tortoises have no predators. They spend their time grazing on grass, leaves, and cacti, sunbathing, and napping—they can snooze for up to 16 hours a day!

VS

★ GALÁPAGOS TORTOISE ★ SEAHORSE

SEAHORSE

❯THEY MAY BE NAMED AFTER A LAND ANIMAL known for its swiftness, but a seahorse isn't a horse—it's one of 38 species of fish that live in warm, shallow waters around the globe. And it's also not swift—in fact, seahorses are some of the slowest swimmers on the planet.

While most fish swim by wiggling their bodies and tails to move through the water, seahorses' only means of locomotion is a puny, fluttering fin on their backs. Other teeny-tiny fins on the sides of their heads are for steering. It can take some kinds of seahorses more than a minute to swim just one foot (31 cm)! We don't mean to judge, but that sure is slow.

Hurry, hurry! THESE SLOWPOKES SEEM LIKE THEY'RE NOT EVEN TRYING TO WIN THIS MATCHUP.

GIANT TORTOISES CAN LIVE SO LONG THAT NO ONE IS SURE EXACTLY HOW LONG. THERE ARE REPORTS OF SOME LIVING **200 YEARS.**

WINNER

GALÁPAGOS TORTOISE

COMMON NAME:	**GALÁPAGOS TORTOISE**	SCIENTIFIC NAME:	**CHELONOIDIS NIGRA**

SIZE:

LONGER THAN
5 FEET (1.5 M)

WHERE THEY LIVE:

ON THE
GALÁPAGOS
ISLANDS IN THE PACIFIC OCEAN

Why are giant tortoises so slow? Because they don't have to be fast! Tortoises have **BUILT-IN ARMOR IN THE FORM OF THEIR HARD SHELLS.** When threatened, the tortoise lets out a hiss as it pushes the air out of its lungs to make itself smaller. Then, it pulls its body inside the safety of its shell.

SLOW INSIDE AND OUT
Tortoises aren't just slow in speed. Their inner workings are slowpokes, too! Giant tortoises have a slow metabolism and are also able to store large amounts of water in their bodies. That gives them the ability to go a really long time without eating or drinking—up to a year!

GIANT VOYAGE
Giant tortoises used to live all over the globe, many on islands separated by hundreds of miles of ocean. How did they get from place to place? Giant tortoises aren't good swimmers. But they are good at bobbing along in a current, long necks stretched high so they can breathe. In this slow but steady manner, these gentle giants conquered the world.

SEAHORSE

| COMMON NAME: | SEAHORSE | SCIENTIFIC NAME: | HIPPOCAMPUS |

SIZE:

0.6 TO 14 INCHES
(1.5–36 CM) LONG

WHERE THEY LIVE:

WARM, SHALLOW
WATERS THROUGHOUT THE WORLD

SEAHORSES CAN MOVE THEIR EYES IN OPPOSITE DIRECTIONS. ONE LOOKS FOR FOOD WHILE THE OTHER WATCHES OUT FOR PREDATORS.

DISAPPEARING ACT

Seahorses can't outswim predators. Instead, they disappear! Most seahorses can change color to blend into their surroundings. The spines and bumps that cover their bodies help them look just like the sponges and coral they're hiding in.

Seahorses are the ultimate **HOMEBODIES. They spend most of their day in the same patch of ocean, with their TAILS WRAPPED AROUND CORAL OR SEA PLANTS, just bobbing along in the current. Sounds relaxing!**

SLOW BUT SNEAKY

Seahorses may be slow, but their prey are incredibly fast: Small crustaceans called copepods that can swim away at speeds of more than 500 body lengths per second—like a person swimming at 2,000 miles an hour (3,200 km/h)! Seahorses' slow speed and body shape allow them to slide through the water without making waves—a slow sneak attack on their speedy prey!

Seahorses sure are slow. Fluttering their feeble fins gets them nowhere fast. One species, the dwarf seahorse, can only move five feet (152 cm) an hour. Imagine trying to get anywhere at that pace! **BUT GALÁPAGOS TORTOISES ARE THE WINNER OF THIS MATCHUP. THEY MIGHT BE SLOW, BUT THEIR LEISURELY LIFESTYLE HAS ALLOWED THEM TO LIVE LONGER THAN HUMANS.** And it's made them world travelers to boot!

EXTREME-LY SLEEPY ANIMALS

THERE'S SLOW... AND THEN THERE'S SNOOZING.

Meet animals that just can't get enough SHUT-EYE.

OPOSSUMS

Opossums are enthusiastic sleepers, **CURLING UP FOR ABOUT 18 HOURS A DAY.** But they take things to the next level: **WHEN STRESSED,** an opossum will enter an involuntary **COMA-LIKE STATE CALLED PLAYING DEAD** that can last up to four hours.

OWL MONKEY

Since it's the only monkey **MOSTLY ACTIVE AT NIGHT,** this tree-dweller **SNOOZES THE DAYLIGHT HOURS AWAY—** about 17 hours each day!

DUCK-BILLED PLATYPUS

Humans get about two hours of REM (rapid eye movement) sleep per night—the stage of sleep when most dreaming occurs. Platypuses put us to shame, logging **EIGHT HOURS OF REM SLEEP** every day! We wonder what they're dreaming about ...

KOALA

These cuddly-looking Australian creatures can **SLEEP UP TO 22 HOURS A DAY** in captivity. That's because koalas eat almost nothing but eucalyptus leaves, which take a lot of energy to digest.

THREE-TOED SLOTH

☑Sloths have a reputation as **LAZY CREATURES.** But do they deserve it? A 2008 study measured the brain waves of wild three-toed sloths and found that they slept much less than scientists expected: **ABOUT 10 HOURS A DAY,** rather than the 15 to 20 observed in captivity.

HOUSE CAT

⌃If you think Fluffy seems like she's always sleeping, you're right. **MOST HOUSE CATS SLEEP BETWEEN 12 AND 16 HOURS A DAY—** twice as much as humans!

GIANT ARMADILLO

◀These South American animals spend as much as **18 HOURS A DAY IN THEIR UNDERGROUND BURROWS.** But since they often build their sleeping chambers next to termite mounds, scientists suspect they're **NOT JUST NAPPING, BUT ALSO EATING.**

BEST HUNTER

THE **KING** OF BEASTS VERSUS A TINY **INSECT**?

There's **MORE** to this matchup than **MEETS THE EYE.**

LION

> **WITH HIS DEAFENING ROAR** and the huge mane encircling his neck, there is no animal more impressive than the mighty lion. Lions live in prides, family groups that usually include about 30 individuals. But even though the males are more fearsome, it's actually female lions that do most of the hunting!

Female lions are smaller than the males—which makes them faster and more agile when it comes to sneaking up on and catching prey. Lionesses hunt everything from insects to antelopes to baby elephants or rhinos, and even crocodiles. They've even been spotted taking down huge animals like African buffalo and giraffes!

DRAGONFLY

❯ THEY BUZZ THROUGH THE SKIES around most of the world. But this common garden insect has a secret: Dragonflies are swift and vicious predators. They appeared on our planet about 300 million years ago—before the dinosaurs!—and they've been perfecting their hunting skills ever since.

Dragonflies are the stealth fighter jets of the insect world. They can zoom in any direction, including sideways or backward, and hover for more than a minute. They don't just chase down their prey: They grab other insects right out of midair, then use their sharp mandibles to rip them apart without even bothering to land. That's fierce!

LION
VS
DRAGONFLY

WHICH ONE OF THESE CREATURES DO YOU THINK IS DEADLIER?

LIONS CAN SLEEP FOR UP TO **21 HOURS** A DAY.

LION

COMMON NAME: **LION**	SCIENTIFIC NAME: **PANTHERA LEO**

SIZE:
MALES CAN BE UP TO
8.3 FEET (2.5 M) LONG

WHERE THEY LIVE:
SUB-SAHARAN
AFRICA AND **INDIA**

A lion chasing down prey **CAN COVER THE LENGTH OF A FOOTBALL FIELD IN SIX SECONDS.** But many of their prey animals, like antelopes, are even faster. So lions have to use the **ELEMENT OF SURPRISE, CONCEALING THEMSELVES IN THE GRASS AND SLOWLY SNEAKING UP** until they're close enough to pounce.

UNDERCOVER
In the daylight hours, lions often sit and watch their potential prey. Then, when night falls, it's time to hunt. Once they choose a victim, lions will stalk it for up to an hour.

TEAMWORK
Bringing down an African buffalo weighing almost 2,000 pounds (900 kg) is a big job. Lionesses often work together to attack large animals. Smaller females will herd their victims toward larger females waiting in the grass to ambush.

DRAGONFLY

COMMON NAME: DRAGONFLY   **SCIENTIFIC NAME:** SUBORDER ANISOPTERA

SIZE:
FROM 0.8 INCHES (2 CM) TO
6 INCHES
(15 CM) ACROSS

WHERE THEY LIVE:
IN
FRESHWATER
HABITATS AROUND THE WORLD

SOME PREHISTORIC DRAGONFLIES WERE **SUPERSIZE,** WITH WINGSPANS THE LENGTH OF A HUMAN ARM.

EYE ON THE PRIZE
A dragonfly's eyes cover almost its entire head. They're made up of 30,000 parts, called facets, that allow the dragonfly to see nearly 360 degrees around it. These eyes are so complex that they can detect colors invisible to humans!

Dragonflies can **REACH SPEEDS OF 30 MILES AN HOUR (48 KM/H) WHILE IN PURSUIT.** And they never seem to get tired of hunting: One scientist watched a dragonfly in her lab **GULP DOWN 30 FLIES IN A ROW, THEN LOOK FOR MORE.**

ALL IN THE HEAD
Dragonflies have a brain center dedicated to hunting. It analyzes the speed and trajectory of a target, predicting where it's going. That means the dragonfly doesn't chase its prey; instead, it flies to the spot where it will be and intercepts it. Usually, the insect has no idea until it's too late.

Lions may be the most feared predator of the African savanna, but the numbers don't lie: Lions are lucky to catch 25 percent of the animals they hunt. That means for every 10 animals they go after, they catch only two or three. Tiny dragonflies, it turns out, are much more skilled. They snag their prey out of the air more than 95 percent of the time. That's a success rate of more than nine out of 10! **SCIENTISTS THINK DRAGONFLIES MAY BE THE PLANET'S BEST HUNTERS. AND THAT MAKES THEM THIS MATCHUP'S WINNER.**

WINNER

EXTREME-LY FEARSOME ANIMALS

Some are ruthless hunters. Others go on offense when they're being hunted themselves. All fight with

WEAPONS *SO* BIZARRE

they're almost unbelievable.

SHRIKE

◄ It looks like a sweet little songbird, but make no mistake: Shrikes don't have powerful talons like eagles—so instead, after they catch a mouse or lizard, they **IMPALE THEIR PREY ON THE SHARP THORNS OF A NEARBY BUSH.**

BOBBIT WORM

◄ Thank goodness these 10-foot (3-m) worms live only on the bottom of the ocean. The worm **BURROWS INTO THE SEAFLOOR,** lying in wait until a meal swims close by—then strikes with **ENOUGH FORCE TO SPLIT A FISH IN TWO!**

TEXAS HORNED LIZARD

If this reptile's sharp **SPIKES AND HORNS** don't send a predator running in the other direction, it has one more **WEAPON** to employ: **IT CAN SHOOT A STREAM OF BLOOD OUT OF ITS EYELIDS!**

BOXER CRAB

These crabs are **ALWAYS CLUTCHING TWO SEA ANEMONES**—one in each claw. They look like cheerleading pom-poms, but the crabs actually use them as **BOXING GLOVES TO DEFEND THEMSELVES** from predators.

SECRETARY BIRD

Africa has some of the most **VENOMOUS SNAKES** on Earth—but they're no match for this bird, which **USES ITS LONG LEGS TO KICK SNAKES TO DEATH.**

BOMBARDIER BEETLE

This insect **EMPLOYS CHEMICAL WARFARE.** When threatened, its body **PUMPS DIFFERENT CHEMICALS,** hydrogen peroxide and hydroquinone, into a **SPECIAL CHAMBER IN ITS REAR END,** where they mix into a **BOILING-HOT, TOXIC SPRAY.**

SMELLIEST

STINKY SPRAYER: **SKUNK** | FOWL ODOR: **HOATZIN**

CAN AN UNKNOWN ANIMAL DEFEAT THE REIGNING CHAMPION IN THIS RIVALRY OF THE MOST REVOLTING?

SKUNK

> **IF YOU SEE THE DISTINCTIVE** black and white coat of a skunk, watch out. That coloring is the first hint that other animals should stay far away. If a predator—or curious dog—ignores this don't-mess-with-me signal, a skunk may stamp its feet in warning. If that, too, is ignored, the skunk will turn, raise its tail, and take aim, releasing a noxious cloud.

The skunk is famous for its awful odor—and it deserves the reputation. Skunks are slow-moving, but when they roam through their territory hunting for insects, mice, and plants, most other animals give them a wide berth. They don't want to be sprayed!

SKUNK VS HOATZIN

HOATZIN

▶ **THIS IS ONE BIZARRE BIRD.** Ever since the hoatzin was discovered in 1776, it's been baffling biologists. It has a mash-up of traits that look like they don't quite belong together: a bright-blue face; a big, round body; and a long tail—all topped with a feathered Mohawk.

Even stranger, hoatzin chicks are born with claws growing from their wings. The birds build their nests over water, and if a hungry monkey comes along looking for a chick snack, the baby leaps into the water to escape. Once the danger has passed, it climbs back up the tree and into the nest using its wing claws. But even that isn't the weirdest thing about the hoatzin. That honor belongs to the bird's odd odor!

WHAT'S THAT SMELL? The winner of this stinky showdown, that's what!

SKUNKS HAVE SENSITIVE **NOSES,** BUT THEY DON'T SEEM TO MIND THEIR OWN ODOR.

Talk about potent! **SKUNK SPRAY** is made of a cocktail of vile-smelling chemicals. Most are thiols, which have **STRONG ODORS RESEMBLING GARLIC OR ROTTEN EGGS.** The stench is so strong it can be **SMELLED A HALF MILE (0.8 KM) AWAY.**

SKUNK

WINNER

WATCH OUT BEHIND
Skunks emit their odor from two glands that rotate independently. On rare occasions, an accurate skunk can hit a target as far as 20 feet (6 m) away.

RINSE AND REGRET
Some chemicals in skunk spray aren't super smelly ... at first. When they touch water, they change form to become much stinkier. That means washing a dog that's been sprayed can actually make the odor worse!

COMMON NAME:	SKUNK	SCIENTIFIC NAME:	MEPHITIS MEPHITIS

SIZE:

UP TO

19 INCHES
(48 CM) LONG, WITH A 15-INCH (38-CM) TAIL

WHERE THEY LIVE:

NORTH

AMERICA

HOATZIN

SHAMEFUL NAME

The hoatzin's belches are said to smell like pungent cow manure. That stench has given the hoatzin its unflattering nickname: the stinkbird.

AWKWARD BIRD

Leaves aren't very nutritious, so hoatzins have to eat a lot. They have supersize digestive systems that take up so much room, there isn't enough space for normal flight muscles. That makes hoatzins clumsy fliers, often barely able to flop from one branch to the next.

The hoatzin is one of the only birds in the world that EATS ALMOST NOTHING BUT LEAVES. To digest all that green stuff, they have a stomach with many chambers—similar to a cow's. Inside these chambers live **BACTERIA THAT DIGEST THE LEAVES, RELEASING METHANE GAS, WHICH THE BIRD THEN BURPS OUT.** Gross!

COMMON NAME:	HOATZIN	SCIENTIFIC NAME:	OPISTHOCOMUS HOAZIN

SIZE:

25.6 INCHES
(65 CM) LONG

WHERE THEY LIVE:

SWAMPY AREAS OF SOUTH
AMERICA

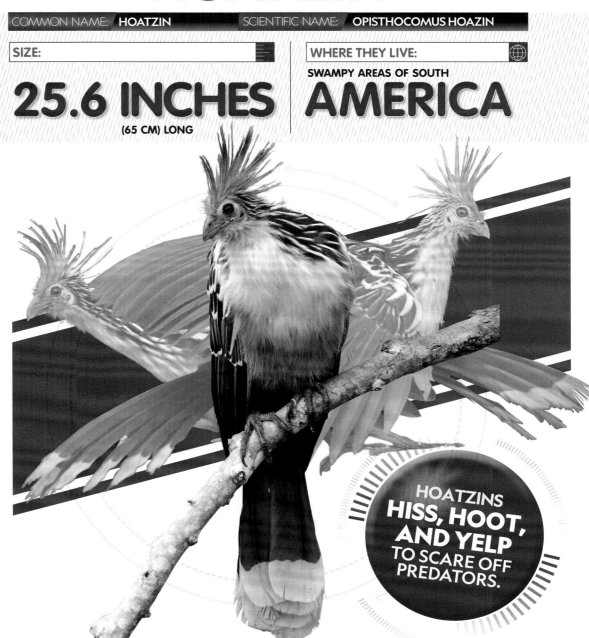

HOATZINS HISS, HOOT, AND YELP TO SCARE OFF PREDATORS.

We wouldn't want to be trapped in a room with either of these animals. While many people have never heard of the hoatzin, a bird that burps is definitely disgusting. But the skunk is legendary in the animal kingdom for its horrible-smelling spray. And it isn't just stinky—the chemicals that give it its odor are so powerful that they're actually flammable. They can even cause temporary blindness! **STINKY WINNER: SKUNK.**

SPIKIEST

QUILL-COVERED: **PORCUPINE** | VENOMOUS AND VICIOUS: **LIONFISH**

KEEP YOUR DISTANCE!

You won't want to mess with these two PRICKLY CREATURES.

PORCUPINE

> **PLUMP AND SLOW-MOVING,** porcupines don't seem very threatening—until you take a closer look and realize that they are covered with thousands of spikes! These natural needles, called quills, are made of bristles of hair fused together. In some species, like Africa's crested porcupine, the quills can be nearly a foot (0.3 m) long!

When a porcupine is mad, it makes its feelings clear. It will stomp its feet, hiss, and shake its quills to let its attacker know it means business. If the animal doesn't back off, a porcupine will charge, smacking the predator with its spiked tail. Many animals walk away from a fight with a porcupine with sharp quills sticking out of its snout. Ouch!

LIONFISH

> **EVERYTHING ABOUT THE LIONFISH SAYS,** "Do not touch!" It has showy zebralike stripes to let other animals know it's venomous. And if those animals ignore the warning and try to snap up a lionfish snack anyway, the spiky fish stings with the spines built into its dorsal fins.

Lionfish don't go out of their way to attack: They eat mainly fish and shrimp, using their lightning-fast reflexes to pounce on unsuspecting swimmers. And they don't have enough venom to make their stings fatal to humans. But if you see one in the ocean, keep your distance: Getting stung by a lionfish is incredibly painful. In the words of one professional diver, "It won't kill you, but it'll make you wish you were dead." Yikes!

PORCUPINE ★ VS ★ LIONFISH

Only one creature can win this battle of the spikiest—
BUT WE WOULD STEER CLEAR OF BOTH!

EACH **QUILL** IS TIPPED WITH A NATURAL ANTIBIOTIC— SO IF A PORCUPINE ACCIDENTALLY SPIKES ITSELF, THE WOUND WON'T GET INFECTED.

PORCUPINE

WINNER

COMMON NAME:	**PORCUPINE**	SCIENTIFIC NAME:	**HYSTRICIDAE**

SIZE:

2.5–4 FEET
(0.8–1.2 M)

WHERE THEY LIVE:

NORTH
AMERICA,
AFRICA, EUROPE, AND ASIA

Porcupines pack a lot of quills: **ABOUT 30,000 OF THEM!** And each of those sharp spikes has spikes of its own: **BETWEEN 700 AND 800 BARBS NEAR THE TIP OF EACH QUILL.**

STUCK ON YOU
Close-up photos of porcupine quills show that they're covered with backward-facing barbs. The porcupine can shed them and walk away, but they stick in its attacker and are very difficult to remove.

STRONG SHOT
Scientists tested the quills' piercing power and found that to penetrate skin, they need 80 percent less force than a hypodermic needle—the kind a doctor uses to give injections! Experts are now studying porcupine quills in the hopes of making shots less painful.

LIONFISH

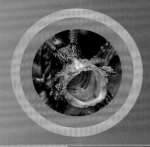

BIG GULP

Lionfish are vicious hunters. They wave their patterned fins to mesmerize their victims, then slurp them up whole! A lionfish's jaw can unhinge to fit an animal nearly its own size.

Lionfish have **FINS MADE OF NEEDLES: UP TO 18 SUPERSHARP SPINES IN TOTAL.** When one of the spines pierces a victim's skin, two glands in its base **RELEASE VENOMS THAT TRAVEL ALONG GROOVES IN THE SPINE** to the puncture wound.

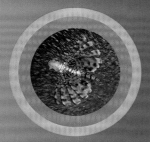

THAT'S FISHY

Lionfish used to only live in the Indian and western Pacific Oceans. But about 25 years ago, a few got into Atlantic waters when people dumped them from their aquariums. Now, they've multiplied into a big problem: A single lionfish can eat nearly 80 percent of all the young fish in its area in just five weeks.

COMMON NAME:	LIONFISH	SCIENTIFIC NAME:	PTEROIS VOLITANS

SIZE:
11.8 TO
15 INCHES
(30 TO 38 CM) LONG

WHERE THEY LIVE:
NATIVE TO THE
INDO-PACIFIC
BUT NOW INVADING ATLANTIC WATERS

GROCERY STORES ARE BEGINNING TO SELL LIONFISH TO TRY TO REDUCE THE NUMBERS OF THIS **INVASIVE** FISH. WOULD YOU TRY THIS **SPINY** SNACK?

Both these animals are super spiky. And lionfish have spines containing venom so toxic it can cause extreme pain in humans! But these prickly animals are invading oceans where they don't belong, gobbling up fish and destroying entire reefs. That makes them come in second in our book. **AND THE WIN GOES TO PORCUPINES!**

NOSIEST

WHICH ONE OF THESE SUPER SNOUTS WILL BE THE VICTOR? WHO NOSE!

SAIGA ANTELOPE

❯ **THIS IS ONE ODD ANTELOPE!** With their gentle, round eyes, ridged horns, and—most of all—their oversize, bulbous noses, saiga antelope look more like cartoon characters than real-life animals. But they are real indeed, roaming the steppes of Central Asia. During the migration season, they join together in herds numbering more than 10,000 to travel hundreds of miles to new grazing areas.

The saiga antelope is an ancient species that once roamed across Europe and North America with saber-toothed cats and woolly mammoths. Today, they are highly endangered, as people hunt them for their horns. They live in some of the harshest lands in the world—and their noses are their secret survival tool.

PROBOSCIS MONKEY

> **THERE IS NO SHORTAGE** of unusual monkeys that swing through the trees on planet Earth. Geladas have red chests. Mandrills have bright red-and-blue faces—and bottoms to match! So it's really saying something that the proboscis monkey might just be the weirdest of them all.

These big-nosed monkeys can only be found in one place: the island of Borneo, in Southeast Asia. They live in groups of about 20, with a male monkey in charge. They eat mainly leaves, which require a lot of digesting. That gives these monkeys another unusual characteristic: big pot bellies to make room for stomachs twice as large as those of any other monkeys of their kind. But that appendage doesn't compare to their superstrange noses.

Read on and SNIFF OUT A WINNER.

A TWO-DAY-OLD SAIGA CAN **OUTRUN** A HUMAN.

SAIGA ANTELOPE

WINNER

| COMMON NAME: | SAIGA ANTELOPE | SCIENTIFIC NAME: | SAIGA TATARICA |

SIZE:

1 TO 2.5 FEET
(31–76 CM) AT THE SHOULDER

WHERE THEY LIVE:

THE STEPPES OF

CENTRAL ASIA

SWELL SMELLER
The saiga's nose isn't just strangely shaped—it's highly flexible. When needed, the antelope can actually inflate its nose, expanding it to super size!

These antelope **TRAVEL** in huge herds across **DRY COUNTRY.** As they go, they **KICK UP A LOT OF CHOKING DUST. BUT THEIR NOSES ACT LIKE FILTERS,** with a system of mucous glands and hairs that **PREVENT TOO MUCH DUST FROM ENTERING THEIR LUNGS.**

BUILT-IN HEATER
The saiga antelope's nose helps it survive in the cold climate where it lives. As cold air travels up the long nose, it heats up. This helps the antelope retain its body heat and keep warm.

PROBOSCIS MONKEY

| COMMON NAME: | **PROBOSCIS MONKEY** | SCIENTIFIC NAME: | **NASALIS LARVATUS** |

SIZE:

22 TO
28 INCHES
(56–71 CM) LONG

WHERE THEY LIVE:

THE SOUTHEAST ASIAN ISLAND OF
BORNEO

TOOT YOUR HORN
It's hard to keep track of your companions in the dense jungle. So proboscis monkeys use their voices to call to each other—and experts believe that their big noses help amplify the sound.

SUPER SNOUT
While all proboscis monkeys have unusual noses, it's only the males that have the truly enormous, dangling kind. Their noses can be up to seven inches (18 cm) long!

THE BIGGER AND STRONGER THE MONKEY, THE BIGGER HIS NOSE TENDS TO BE. Scientists think females use the **LOUDNESS OF A MALE'S CALLS** to judge how attractive he is from a distance.

PROBOSCIS MONKEYS HAVE **WEBBED FEET** THAT HELP THEM **SWIM.**

Neither nose is just for looks: Scientists think the unusual sniffer of the male proboscis monkey helps it attract females. But the saiga antelope's snout does much more than that, allowing the animal to survive in extremely cold weather and make long-distance migrations, too. **THE SAIGA ANTELOPE'S UNIQUE NOSE HAS ALLOWED IT TO LIVE ON OUR PLANET FOR MILLIONS OF YEARS—THAT GIVES IT THE WIN!**

EXTREME-LY NOSE-Y ANIMALS

The animal kingdom's

STRANGEST SNEEZERS, SNIFFERS, AND SNOUTS.

TAPIR

◀ This flexible snout can **SNIFF OUT ODORS** in the dense jungle, **GRAB BRANCHES AND STRIP OFF THE LEAVES—AND EVEN ACT LIKE A SNORKEL** to help the animal breathe when it's underwater!

UNICORNFISH

▼ This ocean-dweller's **HORN BEGINS TO SPROUT BETWEEN ITS EYES WHEN THE FISH REACHES FIVE INCHES** (13 cm) in length. Since the fish uses the sharp spines on its tail for defense, **THE HORN'S FUNCTION IS A MYSTERY!**

ELEPHANT SHREW

▲ If you think this animal's long, trunklike nose really does make it resemble an elephant, you're right! Recent evidence shows that elephant shrews are **CLOSELY RELATED TO A GROUP OF AFRICAN MAMMALS INCLUDING SEA COWS, AARDVARKS— AND ELEPHANTS!**

STAR-NOSED MOLE
⌃ **RINGED BY 22 WIGGLING, FLESHY TENTACLES,** the star-nosed mole's nose is one of the strangest smellers out there. These feelers are incredibly sensitive, allowing the mole to **FIND AND EAT INSECTS AND WORMS IN A QUARTER OF A SECOND.**

NEW WORLD LEAF-NOSED BAT
❮ The bats in this family have a whole assortment of noses: **SOME SQUASHED-LOOKING, SOME STUBBY, SOME LONG AND POINTY.** No one is sure why they have such odd noses, but experts think they may **HELP BATS USE ECHOLOCATION TO NAVIGATE IN THE DARK.**

TOUCAN
It's not just a flashy accessory—the toucan's bill has a **NETWORK OF BLOOD VESSELS CLOSE TO THE SURFACE.** When conditions get hot, the bird **PUMPS BLOOD THROUGH THESE VESSELS, GIVING OFF HEAT TO KEEP ITS BODY COOL.**

THINGS ARE ABOUT TO GET *NASTY!*

An animal named for its habit of **DEALING IN DUNG** versus a **ZOO FAVORITE**. This matchup might surprise you!

DUNG BEETLE

❯**THERE'S NO HIDING THE FACT** that dung beetles are gross—it's right there in the name! Wherever you can find animal poop, you can also find dung beetles. Dung beetles use special antennae to sniff out a whiff of dung. When they sense it, they unfold their long flight wings from under their hard outer ones and take off. They're strong fliers, and some travel miles to find the perfect patty.

When they find the doo-doo they've been looking for, the beetles get down to business. There are three types of dung beetles: rollers, tunnelers, and dwellers. And all of them lead revolting lifestyles.

DUNG BEETLE VS GIRAFFE

GIRAFFE

> **REACHING HEIGHTS** of nearly 20 feet (6 m), a giraffe is tall enough to peer into a second-story window! These spotted, stilt-walking creatures make their home on the African savanna, but they're beloved by people the world over. So why would they enter a competition of Earth's most awful? Well, let's just say this beloved animal of the African savanna is hiding some disgusting secrets.

Even the way giraffes start out their lives is a little startling. Giraffe mothers don't lie down when they give birth. That means a baby giraffe's first experience is dropping from a height of seven feet (2 m) ... headfirst! And that's just the beginning of a lifetime of experiences that one might call a little rude.

WHO'S *REALLY* THE WINNER IN THIS BATTLE?

ANCIENT EGYPTIANS **WORSHIPPED** THE DUNG BEETLE, CALLING IT A **SCARAB.**

DUNG BEETLE

WINNER

| COMMON NAME: | **DUNG BEETLE** | SCIENTIFIC NAME: | **PHANAEUS VINDEX** |

SIZE:

0.2 TO

1.2 INCHES
(0.5–3 CM)

WHERE THEY LIVE:

ON EVERY

CONTINENT
EXCEPT ANTARCTICA

ROLLING ALONG
When a male roller finds a female beetle he likes, he makes her a romantic offering of a giant ball of dung. They roll off into the sunset together until they find the perfect spot where they bury the ball. The female lays her eggs in it, and the dung becomes her baby beetles' first meal.

Tunnelers don't mess around with making dung balls. **THEY DIVE RIGHT INTO A PILE OF DUNG, BURROW DOWN, AND BUILD THEIR FAMILY HOME UNDERNEATH!** That might sound smelly, but this tactic **PROTECTS THE BEETLE LARVAE** from predators.

A DWELLING OF DUNG
Dwellers make their home right on top of the dung heap. The female lays her eggs on the peak of fresh patties, and the babies are born there. Of all the types of droppings on Earth, dwellers seem to like cow patties the best.

GIRAFFE

COMMON NAME:	GIRAFFE	SCIENTIFIC NAME:	GIRAFFA CAMELOPARDALIS

SIZE:

WHERE THEY LIVE:

14–19 FEET
(4–6 M)

AFRICA

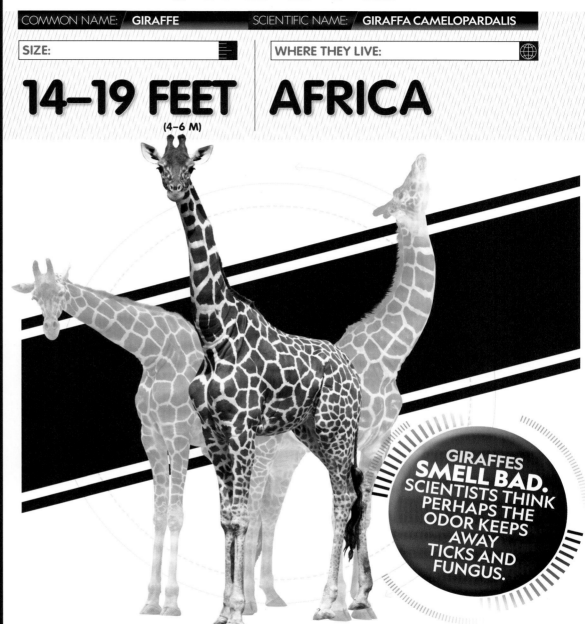

TONGUE TWISTER
Giraffes have an 18-inch (46-cm)-long tongue. Those extra inches help it reach high up into trees to strip off the tasty leaves. Their tongues are also blue-black in color. Scientists think that's to protect them from sunburn!

THE LEAVES OF THE ACACIA TREE ARE A GIRAFFE'S FAVORITE FOOD. But the acacia doesn't want to be eaten. When giraffes come munching, the TREES FILL THEIR LEAVES WITH TOXIC TANNINS. Giraffes fight back— with drool! They release lots of SALIVA THAT NEUTRALIZES THE POISON ... but makes for supermessy eating!

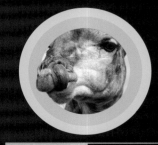

ANT ATTACK
The acacia has another weapon to unleash: ants that attack hungry giraffes in exchange for a place to live in the tree. They crawl into the giraffe's nose and ears, so the giraffe uses its long tongue to scoop them out. Yuck!

GIRAFFES SMELL BAD. SCIENTISTS THINK PERHAPS THE ODOR KEEPS AWAY TICKS AND FUNGUS.

Look down on their lifestyles all you want, but it turns out that dung beetles play a very important role in the health of the planet: They're Earth's janitors. The average cow produces 10 to 12 dung pats per day, and there are 1.5 billion cows on Earth. Dung beetles recycle poop back into the earth—in parts of Texas, U.S.A., for example, it's up to 80 percent! Without these beetles, Earth would be covered in a layer of poop. **THAT GIVES THE BEETLES THE WIN!**

EXTREME-LY
QUESTIONABLE ANIMAL HABITS

If you think skunk spray is bad, get a **FACE FULL** of the

DISGUSTING TACTICS
THESE ANIMALS DEPLOY IN THE NAME OF SELF-PROTECTION.

SEA CUCUMBER

If a predator grabs a sea cucumber in its jaws, it's going to get a nasty surprise. The sea cucumber can **EXPLODE ITS INTERNAL ORGANS OUT OF ITS BEHIND.** That's enough to distract any attacker!

MALAYSIAN ANT

Many ants sting, but the Malaysian ant takes defense to the next level. To protect the rest of the colony, **SOLDIER ANTS WILL SQUEEZE INTERNAL MUSCLES UNTIL POISON-FILLED SACS INSIDE ITS BODY BURST.** The ant explodes, spraying the attacker with its noxious innards.

SONORAN CORAL SNAKE

◀ Some snakes hiss or rattle to scare off predators. Not the Sonoran coral snake. **IT PREFERS TO PASS GAS.** When threatened, it releases air in a popping sound that sounds a lot like human flatulence.

HAGFISH

▼ When it senses a threat, a hagfish deploys its counterattack: It **EMITS SLIME THAT MIXES WITH WATER TO CREATE A THICK GOO** that will cling to a predator's gills and suffocate it until it gives up.

FULMAR

Aww, baby birds are so fluffy and cute. Well, except when **THEY VOMIT UP A STINKING OIL SUBSTANCE FROM THEIR STOMACHS AND SPRAY IT ON PREDATORS** that come too close.

DWARF SPERM WHALE

▶ Like squids, these whales release a dark cloud into the water when threatened. But unlike squids, **THE DWARF SPERM WHALE MAKES ITS CLOUD OUT OF POO.** If that's not bad enough, the whale **THEN USES ITS TAIL TO FAN THE POO CLOUD** all over its attackers.

ODDEST

THIS IS A SHOWDOWN OF THE STRANGE!

It's an **ALIEN-LIKE AMPHIBIAN** up against … what is that, **AN ARTICHOKE?** We're already scratching our heads.

AXOLOTL

> **THERE'S NO DENYING THAT THE AXOLOTL** (pronounced ACK-suh-LAH-tuhl) is weird. This amphibian looks like a creature from another planet. If you saw one crawling across your bedroom in the middle of the night, you'd probably scream!

But with its shy grin, cotton candy pink color, and fringed head-dress, it's also … kind of adorable? That's because unlike other salamanders, axolotls don't ever grow out of their larval stage, and so they retain their gills and tadpole-like appearance for life. Their weird-but-cute appearance has made them beloved by humans. Axolotls make appearances in Mexican art and culture, and they're popular pets in many places around the world, especially Japan.

AXOLOTL VS PANGOLIN

PANGOLIN

> **AT FIRST GLANCE, YOU MIGHT THINK THIS ANIMAL** looks like an anteater wearing medieval armor, or perhaps a pine cone with legs. But it's actually a pangolin, a solitary animal that lives in Africa and Asia. Instead of hair or feathers, pangolins are covered with tough, overlapping scales. They're the only mammals that have them.

When frightened, a pangolin will cover its head with its front legs, showing its scales to the potential predator. If the attacker touches it, the pangolin will roll completely into a ball so tight that it's nearly impossible to unroll. And the scales are so strong that even lions can't bite through them. Good defense!

85

BEWILDERED BY THESE BIZARRE BEASTS? Things are about to get weirder.

THE LAKE WHERE WILD AXOLOTLS LIVE HAS BECOME POLLUTED, AND THE ANIMALS ARE CRITICALLY ENDANGERED.

AXOLOTL

WINNER

| COMMON NAME: **AXOLOTL** | SCIENTIFIC NAME: **AMBYSTOMA MEXICANUM** |

SIZE:

UP TO
12 INCHES
(31 CM) LONG

WHERE THEY LIVE:

IN THE WILD, ONLY IN THE LAKE COMPLEX OF
XOCHIMILCO
(PRONOUNCED SO-CHEE-MILL-KOH) NEAR MEXICO CITY

According to the mythology of the ancient Aztec, Xolotl, the dog-headed god of the underworld, became suspicious that the other gods were going to kill him, so in order to hide, he **TURNED HIMSELF INTO AN AXOLOTL. BUT HE BECAME TRAPPED IN HIS NEW BODY,** doomed to spend the rest of eternity in the lake.

BREATHE RIGHT
The axolotl's odd, feathery headdress isn't for show: It's how the animal breathes! Axolotls flap their fronds around in the water to move away carbon dioxide and mix in oxygen to breathe.

WATCH ME GROW
Many amphibians can regrow lost limbs. But the axolotl takes this ability to another level: These strange creatures can rebuild their jaws, spines ... and even brains! And no matter how many times they do it, the body part comes back perfect each time—something that makes these animals highly unusual.

PANGOLIN

COMMON NAME:	PANGOLIN	SCIENTIFIC NAME:	FAMILY MANIDAE

SIZE:

45 INCHES (114 CM) TO
4.5 FEET
(1.4 M)

WHERE THEY LIVE:
AFRICA AND ASIA

STICK OUT YOUR TONGUE

When fully extended, a pangolin's tongue is longer than its entire body! Unlike most creatures, the pangolin's tongue is connected not in its mouth, but at the bottom of its rib cage. When the tongue is not needed, the pangolin keeps it inside its chest.

PANGOLINS DON'T HAVE TEETH. They use their long claws to tear open ant and termite hills, SLURP UP THE INSECTS WITH THEIR STICKY TONGUES, and swallow them whole. They also eat stones, which help crush up the food in their stomachs.

BECAUSE OF **HUNTING,** THE PANGOLIN IS DANGEROUSLY CLOSE TO **EXTINCTION.**

BACKPACKING

For the first three months of their lives, baby pangolins, called pangopups, hitch a ride—on their mothers' tails! If threatened, the mother pangolin will roll up right around her baby to protect it. Bizarre, but sweet!

Pangolins have been on Earth for 80 million years, they eat about 200,000 ants and termites a day, and, when really scared, they can emit a foul-smelling odor—like skunks! But when they go up against this rare amphibian that breathes with its frilly headgear and can regrow body parts at will, there's really no contest. **AXOLOTLS ARE SO STRANGE—AND ODDLY ADORABLE—THAT WE HOPE THEY DON'T GO EXTINCT. THIS IS ONE WEIRD ANIMAL THAT SHOULD STICK AROUND!**

EXTREME-LY STRANGE CREATURES

THESE ODD ANIMALS SURE ARE WEIRD.

They're also 100 PERCENT REAL.

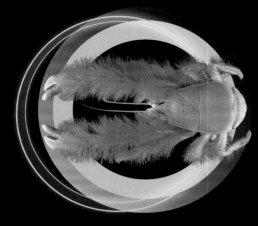

YETI CRAB

THESE EYELESS, HAIRY CRABS LIVE IN one of the world's most extreme environments: **DEEP SEA HYDROTHERMAL VENTS,** which shoot out chemical-filled water reaching temperatures of 750°F (400°C) or higher.

GLASS FROG

Turn a glass frog over so it's belly-up, and you're in for a surprise: **YOU CAN SEE THIS FROG'S INTERNAL ORGANS THROUGH ITS SEE-THROUGH UNDERSIDE!**

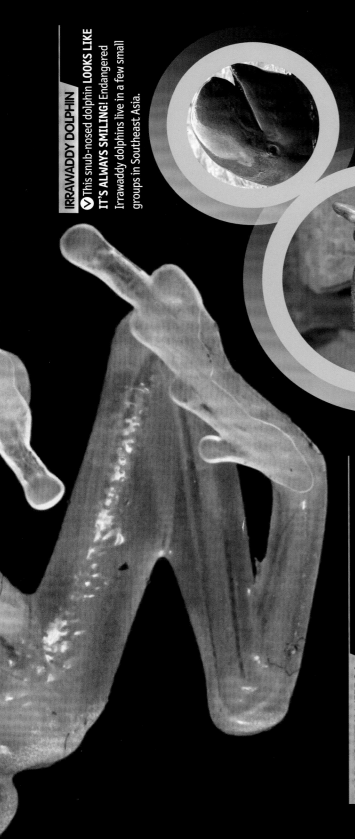

IRRAWADDY DOLPHIN

This snub-nosed dolphin **LOOKS LIKE IT'S ALWAYS SMILING!** Endangered Irrawaddy dolphins live in a few small groups in Southeast Asia.

PINK FAIRY ARMADILLO

Small enough to hold in the palm of your hand, this otherworldly animal has a rosy pink shell framed by wisps of white hair. Pink fairy armadillos **PUMP BLOOD IN AND OUT OF THE SHELL TO CONTROL THEIR BODY TEMPERATURE.**

LESSER EGYPTIAN JERBOA

LOOKING LIKE A MINIATURE KANGAROO, this tiny creature uses its oversize hind legs to hop around the desert sands of North Africa and the Arabian Peninsula. They're so suited for desert life that they **DON'T NEED TO DRINK WATER: THEY CAN GET ALL THEY NEED FROM THEIR FOOD!**

LAMPREY

They don't have jaws, teeth, or bones, but they don't seem to need them: Lampreys have survived on planet Earth for 360 million years! They **LATCH ONTO A HOST WITH THEIR CIRCULAR MOUTH SUCKERS, THEN DRINK ITS BODY FLUIDS.**

MOST LIKELY TO

THESE ANIMALS ARE GOING PLACES!

BIGGEST NEAT FREAK:
CLEANER SHRIMP

MOST LIKELY TO BE A
MOVIE STAR: LYREBIRD

BEST HAIR: ANGORA RABBIT

MOST LIKELY TO BE A MODEL:
JAPANESE SPIDER CRAB

MOST LIKELY TO WIN AN
EATING CONTEST: BLUE WHALE

MOST LIKELY TO HIT THE GYM:
RED KANGAROO

CUTEST COUPLE:
MACARONI PENGUINS

MOST CHANGED:
BLUE MORPHO BUTTERFLY

INDEX

CREDITS

CREDITS

For Dave, my ever-patient test audience. —SWD

Since 1888, the National Geographic Society has funded more than 12,000 research, exploration, and preservation projects around the world. The Society receives funds from National Geographic Partners, LLC, funded in part by your purchase. A portion of the proceeds from this book supports this vital work. To learn more, visit natgeo.com/info.

For more information, visit nationalgeographic.com, call 1-800-647-5463, or write to the following address:

National Geographic Partners
1145 17th Street N.W.
Washington, D.C. 20036-4688 U.S.A.

Visit us online at nationalgeographic.com/books

For librarians and teachers: ngchildrensbooks.org

More for kids from National Geographic: natgeokids.com

National Geographic Kids magazine inspires children to explore their world with fun yet educational articles on animals, science, nature, and more. Using fresh storytelling and amazing photography, *Nat Geo Kids* shows kids ages 6 to 14 the fascinating truth about the world—and why they should care. **kids.nationalgeographic.com/subscribe**

For information about special discounts for bulk purchases, please contact National Geographic Books Special Sales: specialsales@natgeo.com

For rights or permissions inquiries, please contact National Geographic Books Subsidiary Rights: bookrights@natgeo.com

Designed by Fuszion Collaborative, Inc.

Library of Congress Cataloging-in-Publication Data

Names: Drimmer, Stephanie Warren, author. | National Geographic Society (U.S.)
Title: Animal showdown : round two/by Stephanie Warren Drimmer.
Description: Washington, DC : National Geographic Kids,[2019] | Audience: Age 8-12. | Audience: Grade 4 to 6.
Identifiers: LCCN 2018057665| ISBN 9781426334337 (paperback) | ISBN 9781426334344 (hardcover)
Subjects: LCSH: Animals--Juvenile literature.
Classification: LCC QL49 .D75 2019 | DDC 590--dc23
LC record available at https://lccn.loc.gov/2018057665

The publisher would like to thank everyone who helped make this book possible: Ariane Szu-Tu, editor; Brett Challos, art director; Shannon Hibberd, senior photo editor; Marti Davila and Rick Heffner at Fuszion; Kristin Sladen, freelance photo editor; Molly Reid, production editor; Scott Vehstedt, fact-checker; and Gus Tello and Anne LeongSon, design production assistants.

Printed in China
19/RRDS/1